LAND OF THE FESTIVALS

An Introduction to Indian Culture and Traditions

SHOEBILL

www.shoebill.com

ISBN: 978−1−949002−19−5

I dedicate this book to my daughter Riya. She was born in the United States and I want her to be aware of the rich cultural traditions and festivals that I grew up with, so that her roots are not forgotten. I would like thank my family for their constant support that they have given me throughout.

About India

India is the 7th largest country in the world by land size with a total population of 1.4 Billion people as of 2020. It is one of the oldest civilization in the world with a polychromatic variety and rich cultural heritage. India is often referred to as the "Land of the Festivals". One of India's famous writer Siddharth Katragadda quotes "The Greatness of a Culture can be found in its Festivals" so the greatness of India can be examined by glancing upon the wide variety of festivals celebrated which makes it a true manifestation of its rich culture and traditions. It is highly a spiritual country which makes festivals at the heart of people's lives in India. The numerous and distinct festivals that are celebrated throughout the year provides a very unique way of experiencing Indian culture at its best. It is perhaps the only country where every religion and community celebrate their culture. These festivals are often categorized as state wise, religion based and community based.

This book provides a brief introduction on the major festivals of India, its significance and the attractions. Millions of tourists from around the world visit India and are able to have a blissful experience of the Indian festivals and allowing them an opportunity to meet the local people and witness the country at its vibrant best. While there are many different festivals and celebrations, we will cover the most celebrated ones in this book. Each festival will be introduced in the order in which they occur throughout the calendar year starting from January all the way till December!

INDIA

Makar Sankranti

Makar Sankranti is the first festival of the year celebrated each year on 14th January, taking place after the winter solstice when the sun transitions back to the northern hemisphere. It marks the end of the winter and the start of warmer weather and the new harvest season for farmers. The event takes place each year on the day that the sun enters the zodiac sign of Capricorn or Makar. It is celebrated all over India but with different names in different states. The festival is known as Makar Sankranti in West India, Pongal in South India and Lohri in North India. Uttarayan, Maghi, & Khichdi are some other names of the same festival.

People celebrate this festival by flying kites and enjoy a savory of 'Til Ladoo' which is a sweet ball of Sesame seeds.

Significance: Beginning of agricultural cycle

Attractions: Kite Flying

Vasant Panchami

Vasant Panchami also called as Basant Panchami, is a festival that marks the preparation for the arrival of spring. It is the festival dedicated to goddess Saraswati who is the goddess of knowledge, language, music and all arts. On this day, people dress in yellow as yellow is the favorite color of goddess Saraswati and they offer yellow flowers to others and to the gods and goddesses. India's crop fields are filled with the color yellow, as the yellow mustard flowers bloom at this time of the year.

Significance: It marks the beginning of Spring.

Attractions: People wear yellow-colored clothes and make yellow dishes like sweet Saffron rice and Curry.

Maha Shivratri

Maha Shivratri, which translates to "Great Night of Shiva" is a Hindu festival largely celebrated in India as well as in Nepal. The festival is celebrated on the new moon day in the month of Maagha (either January or February) according to the Hindu calendar. The day is celebrated to venerate Lord Shiva, an important deity in Hindu culture. People often fast on the night of Shivratri and sing hymns and praises in the name of Lord Shiva. Temples across the country are decorated with lights and colorful decorations and people can be seen offering night long prayers to Shiva Lingam. It is believed that the people who fast on this night and offer prayers to Lord Shiva bring good luck into their life.

Significance: Devotion to Lord Shiva

Attractions: Fasting and worshipping Lord Shiva

Holi

Holi is one of the most famous festival of India. It is known as the festival of colors. On the eve of Holi, people around the country make huge Holika bonfires and sing and dance around it. On the day of Holi, people come out in open areas and apply dry and wet colors of multiple hues to each other, with some carrying water guns and colored water-filled balloons. There is a legend of Prahlad and Hiranyakshyap behind Holi. The legend goes on as - there once lived a devil and powerful king, Hiranyakshyap who considered himself a god and wanted everybody to worship him. To his great ire, his son, Prahlad began to worship, Lord Vishnu. To get rid of his son, Hiranyakshyap asked his sister, Holika to enter a blazing fire with Prahlad in her lap, as she had a boon to enter fire unscathed. Legend has it that Prahlad was saved for his extreme devotion for the lord while Holika paid a price for her sinister desire. Holika wasn't aware her boon only worked when she entered the fire alone. The tradition of burning Holika or the 'Holika dahan' comes mainly from this legend.

Significance: It signifies the victory of good (Prince Prahlad) over evil (Holika) and the arrival of spring.

Attractions: Holika bonfire, playing with colors.

Baisakhi

Baisakhi also known as Vaisakhi or Vaishakhi, is a religious festival mainly in Sikh religion. It is one of the most famous festivals of India. It celebrates the welcoming of the harvest season for the rabi crops. The Sikhs celebrate this festival with a lot of excitement and enthusiasm by performing local folk dances such as Bhangra. It marks the Sikh New Year and commemorates the formation of Khalsa panth of warriors under Guru Gobind Singh in 1699.

Significance: Welcome the arrival of the harvest season

Attractions: Folk dance like Bhangra and Gidda, decorations in houses and Gurudwaras (temple of the Sikhs).

Bihu

Bihu is a popular festival celebrated mainly in the North East of India especially in the state of Assam. It is referred to as the harvest festival of Assam and marks the shift in the Sun's solstice. It is a month-long celebration where young men and women wear traditional clothes and perform the Bihu dance in the fields and courtyards. A community feast is held during Bihu celebration with a lot of fanfare. There are set of three Bihu festivals: Rongali celebrated in April, Kongali celebrated in October and Bhogali celebrated in January. Rongali Bihu is the most important of the three commemorating the Assamese New Year and spring festival.

Significance: New Year celebration of the State of Assam

Attractions: The Bihu dance and the local cuisine

Easter

Easter commemorates the resurrection of Jesus Christ from the dead. India is a land of cultural diversity; hence Easter is also celebrated with great zeal and enthusiasm throughout India. Easter is one of the most significant festivals in the Christian calendar and marks the beginning of the spring season. The major followers of Christianity in India, fall in the city of Mumbai, southern states like Goa, Pondicherry, and Kerala and North-eastern States like Mizoram, Meghalaya, and Nagaland. The churches are decorated and filled with cheer and joy during this time of the year. Easter celebrations in India are distinguished by various colorful decorations, dance and plays, simmel and plum cakes, and bright lanterns adorning the streets.

Significance: Resurrection of Lord Jesus

Attractions: Folk songs and dance, Easter eggs, cakes, chocolates, street decorations.

Buddha Jayanti

Buddha Jayanti or Buddha Purnima is observed on the full moon of the month of Vaisakh (April/May). It is also known as Vesakha, Buddha Day or Buddha's birthday. The festival marks the day when Lord Buddha, the founder of Buddhism was born, attained enlightenment and got Moksha (liberation from cycles of rebirth). Followers of Buddhism all over the world celebrate this festival and many Hindus also celebrate the festival. It is said that Buddha attained enlightenment in Bodh Gaya, a town in the Indian state of Bihar. In order to make the most of this day, people indulge themselves in attending Buddhist teachings and wear white clothes to follow the tradition.

Significance: People celebrate this festival as Gautama Buddha was born on this day

Attractions: People impart the teachings of Buddhism and everyone wears white clothes

Eid–Ul–Fitr

Eid is one of the major festivals of India for the Muslim community. It is also called as Ramadan Id in India. Eid, means festivity after breaking the fast. Eid is celebrated at the end of Ramadan, the holy month of fasting in Islam, A month of fasting when people don't eat and drink during the day. The three-day festival of breaking of the fast occurs when the new moon is sighted. People dress up in traditional dresses, attend a special community prayer in the morning, visit friends, and relatives and exchange sweets. Children are given idi (money or gift) by elders.

Significance: It celebrates the conclusion of the holy month of fasting called Ramadan.

Attractions: The beautifully decked up markets and mosques, the morning Eid namaz at the mosques, and the sweet dishes including Sheer Khurma, Seviyaan with dates.

Raksha Bandhan

One of the most famous festivals in the list is the festival of Raksha Bandhan or Rakhi. It celebrates the bond of protection between brothers and sisters. The word Raksha means protection, whilst Bandhan is the verb to tie. It is an occasion to nourish love, care, and sacred feeling of brotherhood. Raksha Bandhan is mainly celebrated in the northern and western region of India. Sisters tie Rakhi (a sacred thread) on the wrist of their brothers between chanting of mantras whilst applying Tilak (red color spot) and rice on his forehead as a mark to win against life circumstances. There is an exchange of gifts, symbolizing the physical acceptance of her love and his pledge towards togetherness and protecting her.

Significance: It symbolizes the strong bonding of a brother and sister.

Attractions: Rakhis are often decorated with multi-colored silk thread, and often adorned with stones and beads.

Janmashtmi

Janmashtami is one of the most important religious festivals of India. The festival is a celebration of the birth of Lord Krishna, eight Avatar of Lord Vishnu. Janmashtami means the birth on the eighth day of the dark fortnight in the Krishna Paksha of the Hindu Calendar. The Bhagavad Gita, a holy book for the Hindus is a preaching given by Lord Krishna to Arjuna, one of the Pandavas who was in a state of distress and confusion at the time of the Mahabharata. The number eight plays a big role, not only because of the Ashtami, but also because Lord Krishna was the eighth incarnation of Lord Vishnu, he was also the eighth child of Devaki.

People celebrate this day by fasting throughout the day and break it with a special meal after dusk. People visit temples, pray, dance and sign bhajans (hymns) at midnight as part of the celebrations of the birth of Lord Krishna. Often, small children dress up like Lord Krishna on this day. Pictures and plays of Krishna's life story are depicted in temples. Dahi Handi, a team sport is played where young boys form a human pyramid to break the earthen pot hanging at the top containing buttermilk. Dahi Handi is celebrated a day after Janmashtmi.

Significance: It is the annual celebration of the birthday of Lord Krishna.

Attractions: Singing of the hymns in temples, Dahi Handi.

Onam

Onam is famous festival of India and is mainly celebrated in the southernmost state of Kerala, which is also referred to as God's own country. According to the legends, Mahabali was the great great grandson of Kashyapa and was an ardent devotee of Lord Vishnu. Once Vishnu decided to test Mahabali by taking the form of a dwarf boy called Vamana. Mahabali had announced that he would be performing Yajna (home sacrifice) and grant anyone any request. Vamana claimed that one should not ask for more than they needed and only asked for 3 footsteps of land and Mahabali agreed. Vamana grew extremely big and covered whatever Mahabali owned in two steps. As for the third step, Mahabali offered himself an act which was accepted as devotion for Vishnu. Hence, Vishnu gave a boon to Mahabali according to which Mahabali could visit his land and people once every year. This visit of Mahabali marks Onam, a reminder of his prosperous rule and his humility in front of the Lord Vishnu.

On this day, people wear traditional wear, adorn houses with floral designs, and prepare elaborate meals. Events such as snake boat race, clap dance, Kathakali dance, and Pulikali procession (artists dressed and painted like tigers and hunters) are held.

Significance: It celebrates the homecoming of the legendary king Mahabali.

Attractions: The spectacular Snake Boat Race, the enigmatic Kaikottikali dance, and the Elephant procession where elephants wear ornaments and jewelry.

Ganesh Chaturthi

Ganesh Chaturthi is a ten-day festival and one of the major Hindu festivals of India. The festival celebrates the birth of the elephant headed deity Ganesha who is believed to be the most revered gods of Hindu mythology. Ganesha is the son of Lord Shiva and goddess Parvati. Ganesha is the god of prosperity, knowledge, wisdom and good luck. The idols of Ganesha are beautifully decorated and adorned with jewels, and different prayers are sung worshipping the idol.

Ganesha is believed to be the "Vigana Harta" meaning the one who can remove all the existing problems in life. People pray to Ganesha before performing any activity to be blessed with good luck.

Significance: It's the birthday of Lord Ganesha, the elephant-headed God.

Attractions: Beautifully crafted life size idols of Ganesha, and the immersion ceremony.

Navratri

Navratri means "nine nights" in Sanskrit is one of the most famous festivals of India. It is also called as Durga Puja in honor of "Goddess Durga". During these nine nights and ten days, nine forms of Shakti / Devi are worshiped. Navratri occurs over 9 days during the month of Ashvin (September–October). The festival's nine nights are dedicated to different aspects of the divine feminine principle, or shakti. While the pattern varies somewhat by region, generally the first third of the festival focuses on aspects of the goddess Durga, the second third on the goddess Lakshmi, and the final third on the goddess Sarasvati.

This festival is celebrated by all people throughout India in different ways. In the state of Gujarat, it is a nine-day celebration of rejuvenating Garba nights and highly energetic Dandiya-Raas dances. People are dressed in beautiful, colorful traditional clothes and the environment is very youthful and invigorating. Fasting is observed during all the nine days of the festival.

Significance: The festival symbolizes the victory of good over evil

Attractions: 9 days of dance festivities in Gujarat and every temple to Goddess Durga are beautifully decorated with flowers, leaves and petals and Idols of Goddess Durga are highly ornated.

Durga Puja

Durga Puja celebrates the victory of Goddess Durga over the demon Mahishasur. It is celebrated for a period of 10 days. Durga Puja coincides with the same dates of Navaratri and Dussehra. It celebrates the victory of the ten-armed Goddess Durga over the deceptive buffalo demon Mahishasur, which falls on the same day of Dussehra. Tourists from all over the world visit West Bengal to experience the joyful occasion in the City of Joy itself and the tenth day of the occasion is Vijayadashami or Dussehra which symbolizes the end of the grand festival.

Significance: Celebrate the victory of good over evil on the joyous occasion of Durga Puja festival.

Attractions: Beautiful ten-armed Durga idols.

Dussehra

Dussehra festival is ten days long, and it marks the tenth day of the Navaratri Festival. It is also referred to as Vijayadashami, It is mainly devoted to celebrating the defeat of the Evil king Ravana by Lord Rama deciphered from the holy Hindu text The Ramayana.

According to Ramayana, Surpanakha, the sister of Ravana, fell in love with Rama and Lakshman, and wanted to marry any one of them. After being refused by both, she threatened them to kill Sita who was Rama's wife. Lakshman, in anger, cut her ears and nose. This led to Ravana abducting Sita in order to take revenge of her sister. To rescue Sita, Rama and Lakshmana fought a battle with Ravana in present day Sri Lanka. Lord Hanuman and an enormous army of monkeys helped the brothers. Ultimately, Rama defeated Ravana and this day is celebrated on the victory of the good over the evil. The word Dussehra comes from two Sanskrit words dasha (symbolizing the ten heads of Ravana) and hara, which means 'to defeat', burning the effigies of Ravana.

Significance: Celebration of the victory of Rama over the Evil King Ravana.

Attractions: Burning of the effigies of the ten headed Ravana.

Diwali

Diwali is the Grandest of all festivals in India. It is the Festival of Lights and the most well-known festival around the world. It is celebrated with a lot of pomp and show. During this festival of lights, houses are decorated with clay lamps and candles. People wear new clothes, participate in family prayers, burst fire-crackers, and share sweets with friends, families, and neighbors. It's a 5 days long celebrated festival starting with Dhanteras and ending with BhaiDooj. People worship Goddess Lakshmi who symbolizes wealth and prosperity, and her blessings are invoked for a good year ahead.

Significance: The festival marks the return of Lord Rama, along with his wife Sita and brother Lakshman, after a long exile of 14 years.

Attractions: Homes are decorated with clay lamps, fancy lights and candles. People burst fire-crackers all evening on that day

Guru Nanak Jayanti

Guru Nanak Jayanti also known as Gurpurab, is the celebration of the birth of the first Sikh guru, Shri Guru Nanak Dev Ji. It the birth anniversary of the first guru of Sikhs, which makes this day very sacred for the Sikh community. The day begins with early morning prayers at the sacred place of Sikhs, which is the gurudwara. The celebration of this day begins two days prior by reading the holy book which is called Guru Granth Sahib (Guru means Teacher, Granth means Sacred Book and Sahib means Lord), for straight two days or forty-eight hours in the gurudwaras. The gurudwaras are decorated beautifully during this time especially, the Golden Temple at Amritsar. Langars (community meals) are organized in the gurudwaras. Karah Prasad (sweet) is distributed among all, and hymn chanting processions are held in the city.

Significance: It is the celebration of the anniversary of the ten Sikh Gurus

Attractions: Singing of Bhajan-Kirtan (hymns), Gurbani in the Gurdwaras, the Langar and the Karah Prasad

Christmas

Christmas is one of the biggest festivals of the world, the holiday season is celebrated grandly in the west to worship the day Jesus Christ was born on 25th December. India being a secular nation, is a home to all religions and Christianity is a huge part of this diverse cultured nation for it is the third most followed religion in India. Many Catholics and Non-Catholics celebrate this festival with great enthusiasm all throughout India. The secularist people of India, all look forward to the 25th of December every year and wait for the arrival of Santa Claus who brings bunch of gifts. There are Christmas masses, some in the morning, some in the night. The festival is vastly celebrated in the Southern and Northeastern parts of the country. Goa is known to be the best place to be in India on the days of Christmas.

Significance: Birth of Jesus Christ

Attractions: Christmas tree decoration, prayers, Santa Claus.

www.ingramcontent.com/pod-product-compliance
Lightning Source LLC
LaVergne TN
LVHW072118070426
835510LV00003B/111